WONDERFUL CHRISTMAST

ISBN 0-7935-1747-8

A Publication of

MPL COMMUNICATIONS, INC.

Distributed by

Hal Leonard Publishing Corporation

7777 West Bluemound Road P.O. Box 13819 Milwaukee, WI 53213

A CAROL
(From "THE BALLAD OF JOHNNY POT")

Lyric by CAROLYN RICHTER
Music by CLINTON BALLARD

CHRISTMAS IS A-COMIN'
(MAY GOD BLESS YOU)

Words and Music by FRANK LUTHER

THE CHRISTMAS SONG
(CHESTNUTS ROASTING ON AN OPEN FIRE)

Music and Lyric by MEL TORME
and ROBERT WELLS

Sentimentally

CHRISTMAS MAGIC
(THE MEANING OF CHRISTMAS)

Words and Music by MARK LAWRENCE

⊕ OPTIONAL ENDING

Christ - mas ma - gic comes from year 'round lov-ing, That's how

Cm   Abm   Gm7   F7   Fm7-5

rit. *Freely ad-lib.*

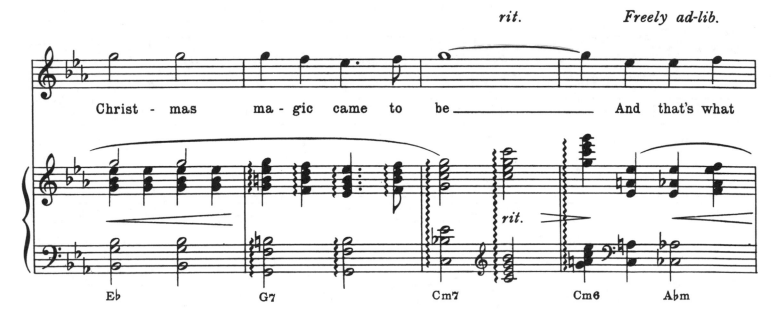

Christ - mas ma - gic came to be _____ And that's what

Eb   G7   Cm7   Cm6   Abm

rit. *a tempo* *rit.*

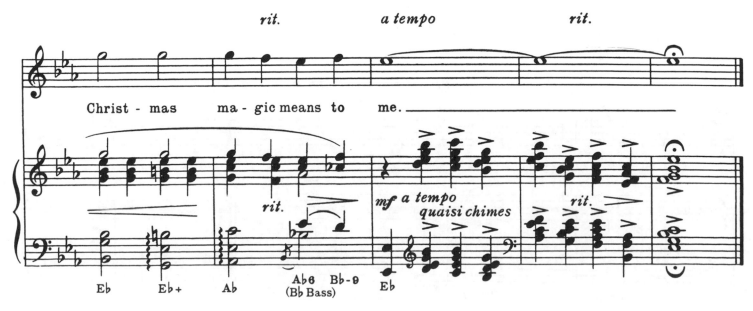

Christ - mas ma - gic means to me. _____

Eb Eb+   Ab   Ab6 Bb-9   Eb
                  (Bb Bass)

I WANT A HIPPOPOTAMUS FOR CHRISTMAS
(HIPPO THE HERO)

Words and Music by
JOHN ROX

13

IT'S BEGINNING TO LOOK LIKE CHRISTMAS

In a Moderate Tempo

Words and Music by MEREDITH WILLSON

18

MAY THE GOOD LORD BLESS AND KEEP YOU

Words and Music by MEREDITH WILLSON

21

JINGLE BELLS

J. PIERPONT

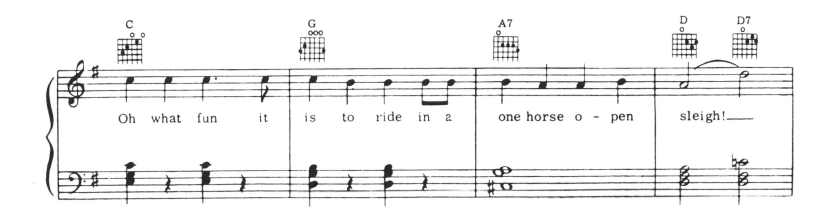

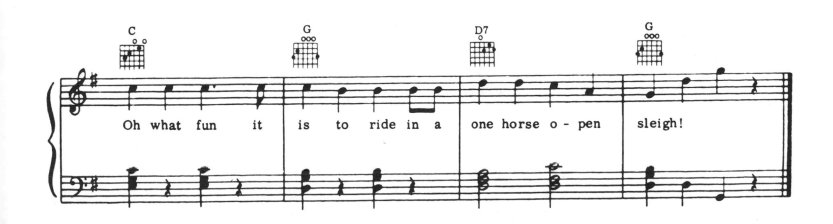

LET'S HAVE AN OLD FASHIONED CHRISTMAS

Lyric by LARRY CONLEY
Music by JOE SOLOMON

*Symbols for Guitar, Ukulele and Banjo

25

MISTER SANTA

Words and Music by PAT BALLARD

MY CHRISTMAS SONG FOR YOU

Lyric by FURNISS PETERSON and PAUL FRANCIS WEBSTER
Music by HOAGY CARMICHAEL

My Christ - mas song for you is all the old things tried and true, like jin - gle bells and chest - nut dells, a

31

MY WISH

(From "HERE'S LOVE")

Words and Music by
MEREDITH WILLSON

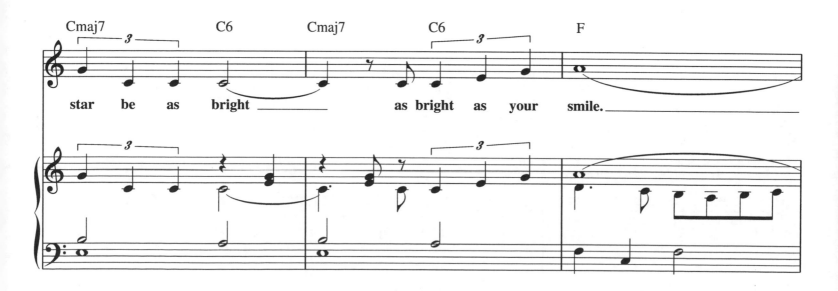

34

O CHRISTMAS TREE

OLD GERMAN CAROL

Not too slow

O Christ-mas Tree, O Christ-mas Tree, You stand in ver-dant beau-ty! O

Christ-mas Tree, O Christ-mas Tree, You stand in ver-dant beau-ty! Your

boughs are green in sum-mer's glow, And do not fade in win-ter's snow. O

Christ-mas Tree, O Christ-mas Tree, You stand in ver-dant beau-ty!

O LITTLE TOWN OF BETHLEHEM

PHILLIPS BROOKS

LEWIS H. REDNER

2. For Christ is born of Mary,
   And gathered all above,
   While mortals sleep, the angels keep
   Their watch of wondering love.
   O morning stars, together
   Proclaim the holy birth,
   And praises sing to God the King,
   And peace to men on earth.

3. How silently, how silently,
   The wondrous gift is giv'n!
   So God imparts to human hearts
   The blessings of His heav'n.
   No ear may hear His coming,
   But in this world of sin,
   Where meek souls will receive Him still,
   The dear Christ enters in.

PINE CONES AND HOLLY BERRIES
(From "HERE'S LOVE")

Words and Music by MEREDITH WILLSON

SILENT NIGHT

JOSEPH MOHR

FRANZ GRUBER

Reverently

1. Si - lent night! Ho - ly night! All is calm, all is bright. Round you Vir - gin Moth - er and Child! Ho - ly In - fant so ten - der and mild, Sleep in heav - en - ly peace,_____ Sleep___ in heav - en - ly peace._____

2. Silent night! Holy night!
Shepherds quake at the sight!
Glories stream from heaven afar,
Heav'nly hosts sing Alleluia,
Christ, the Saviour, is born!
Christ, the Saviour, is born!

3. Silent night! Holy night!
Son of God, love's pure light
Radiant beams from Thy holy face,
With the dawn of redeeming grace,
Jesus, Lord at Thy birth,
Jesus, Lord at Thy birth.

SOME THINGS FOR CHRISTMAS
(A SNAKE, SOME MICE, SOME GLUE AND A HOLE TOO)

Lyric by JACQUELYN REINACH
and JOAN LAMPORT
Music by JACQUELYN REINACH

47

THIS IS THAT TIME OF THE YEAR

Lyric by MARTIN CHARNIN
Music by EDWARD THOMAS

50

THE TWELVE DAYS OF CHRISTMAS

TRADITIONAL

WE NEED A LITTLE CHRISTMAS
(From "MAME")

Music and Lyric by JERRY HERMAN

Brightly (as a polka)

WE THREE KINGS OF ORIENT ARE

JOHN H. HOPKINS

WHAT ARE YOU DOING NEW YEAR'S EVE?

Slowly and sentimentally

Words and Music by FRANK LOESSER

WONDERFUL CHRISTMASTIME

Words and Music by McCARTNEY

62

MERRY CHRISTMAS!